YOUNG MASTERS

This Little Light

Written by Bunny Hull

Illustrations by Kye Fleming

Edited by Wendy Werris

Layout & Typography by James Suelflow

ISBN 978-0-9826278-1-5

Little Wisdom Series
© 2010 Dream A World®

www.dreamaworld.com

Once upon a time, somewhere over the sky and under the moon, Butaan, Phylos and EEtha set foot on planet Earth for the very first time. Until then they had only heard stories about the powerful gifts born to the people of Earth.

Now they would learn all about them. What were the gifts? How were they used? It was there in a magic garden that their adventures began, as they sat by the stream and talked about the very important things they learned from Saphinne – *the secrets of the heart*.

"Look at all these little fireflies," said Phylos.
"How do you think they light up like that?"

"Something must make them glow," said EEtha.

"Do you think everyone on Earth has a light that shines?" asked Phylos.

"Saphinne says that the people of Earth are born with an inside light that shines all the time," said Butaan.

"An inside light?" asked Phylos.
"What's that called?"

"Saphinne says it's called love,"
said Butaan.

"What's love?" asked EEtha.

"It's a feeling you have about someone that makes you warm and happy," said Butaan.

"What happens when you love someone?" asked EEtha.

"You feel your love light get very bright," said Butaan, "kind of like you swallowed the sun and it tickles your tummy and makes you smile a lot."

"How do you know who you're supposed to love?" asked Phylos.

"It's one of the secrets your heart tells you," said Butaan.

"It happens a lot in families, and with friends and teachers,
 but some people just love everyone."

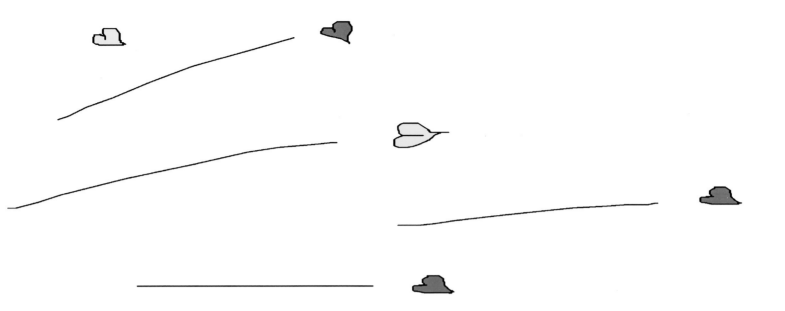

"What do you do when you love someone?" asked EEtha.

"Saphinne says the best thing is just to let your light out and shine it as big you can," said Butaan.

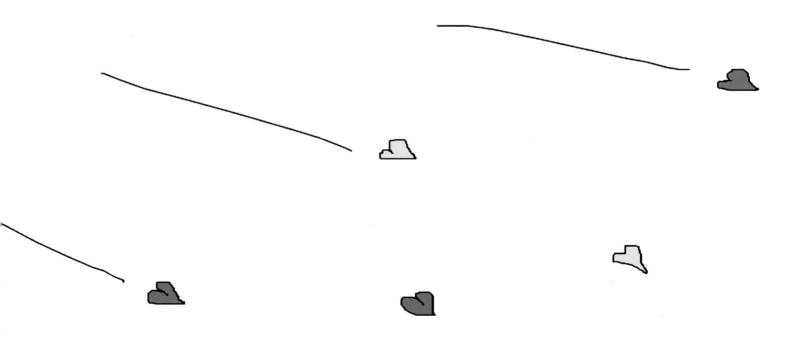

"How do you do that?" asked Phylos.

"By thinking good thoughts and saying nice things," said Butaan, "and by taking care of those you love."

"Maybe you could give them a really tight hug," said Phylos.

"Or make a special gift for them," said EEtha.

"Saying *I love you* would be something good to do," said Butaan.
"How else would they know, if you didn't tell them?"

"Are there different kinds of love?" asked Phylos.

"Well," said Butaan, "Saphinne says sometimes people fall in love, and when that happens they feel like two peas in a pod, and they want to hold hands all the time."

"Can you love other things besides people?" asked EEtha.

"Earth people love their pets and other animals very much," said Butaan, "and their animals love them too."

"People love all kinds of things, like playing an instrument, or reading," said Butaan.

"Or maybe they love the color purple," said Phylos.

"How about the Earth?" asked EEtha. "Do they love it?"

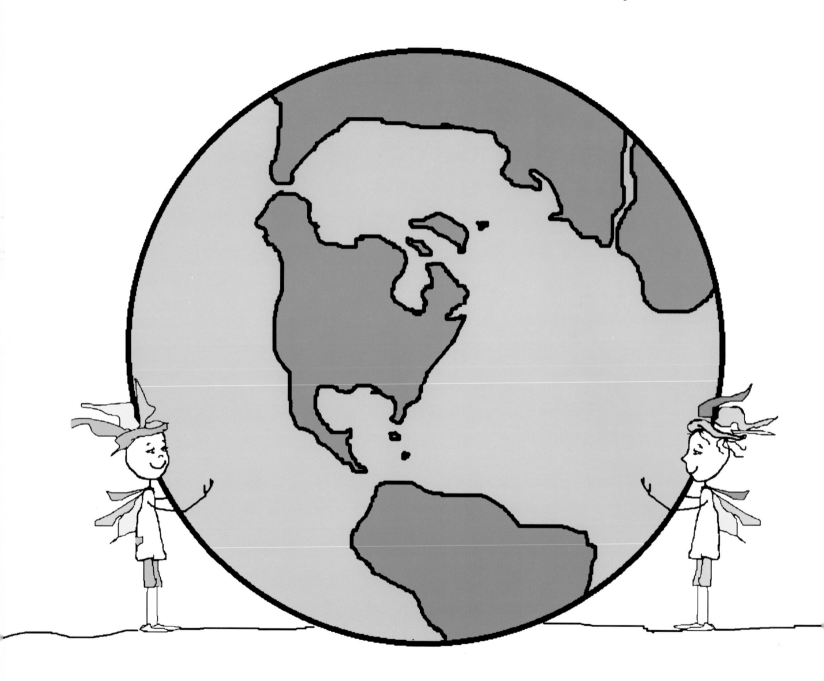

"Saphinne says loving the Earth is very important," said Butaan.

"How do you love a planet?"
asked Phylos.

"By taking care of it,"
said Butaan.

"And how do you know when someone loves you?" asked EEtha.

"They make you feel safe," said Butaan, "and they'd do almost anything for you."

"If you love yourself," giggled Phylos,
"does your love light shine brighter?"

"Oh yes," said Butaan, "When you love yourself you have even more love to give."

"And Saphinne says when you give love, it goes around in a circle and comes right back to you."

"All you have to do is sprinkle a little love light," said Butaan,
"and love pops up everywhere!"

"Love makes the world beautiful," said EEtha.

Have you told someone you love them today?

Thank you for being here!

Download the song lyrics and activity pages at www.dreamaworld.com

"The Young Master's Pledge," "Here We Go," "This Little Light – Story," "I Love Everybody,"
"When You Share Love," "This Little Light," "Love Goes Around In A Circle," "Hey Young Master,"
"What Can I Learn Today," "Thank You For Being Here," "Asanti Ku kuwa Hapa" (Swahili),
All songs produced, written and performed by Bunny Hull
Except "This Little Light" and "I Love Everybody" – Traditional – Arranged by Bunny Hull

"Asanti Ku kuwa Hapa" - Swahili Translation by Anindo Marshall

"Young Masters Pledge" and "This Little Light – Story" are narrated by by Elayn J. Taylor

Flute: Diane Hsu * Guitar: James Harrah * Ukulele: Steve Rose
Percussion and Additional vocals: Anindo Marshall
Children's background vocals: Jadah Fahnbulleh & Saamera Jamai
Additional percussion: Jeff Hull * Multimedia voiceovers: Lauren Wood

Recorded by Bunny Hull
Mixed by Jeff Hull at Dream A World Studios
Mastering: Dwarf Village Studios, Valley Village

Dedicated to my father, my teachers and the many friends who share and
support my vision for children everywhere…especially Char and IPA.

ISBN 978-0-9826278-1-5

Little Wisdom Series
© 2010 Dream A World®

www.dreamaworld.com

Bunny Hull – Author, Songwriter

A resident of Los Angeles, California, Hull is a Grammy Award®-winning songwriter and recipient of over 20 Gold and Platinum albums, with songs that have appeared on television and in films which include *The Prince Of Egypt, Bruce Almighty, Sesame Street, Oprah, The Simpsons* and *Evan Almighty.*

In the world of children's books and music, Hull is the recipient of a Parents' Choice Award, Three National Parenting Publication Awards, two Dr. Toy Awards and a Parent's Guide To Children's Media Award. Hull's non-profit, Dream A World Education, Inc. currently serves children in the Los Angeles area, using music and the arts to empower children 4 – 7 to learn about self-image, diversity, relationships and the universal principles that join us as a global family.

Kye Fleming – Illustrator

A Nashville, Tennessee resident, Fleming comes from the music world where she has established a career as an award-winning songwriter; three time BMI Writer of the Year; and Grammy, CMA, ACM and Dove nominee. Other awards include Billboard Song of the Year and in 2009 she was inducted into the Nashville Songwriter Association International Songwriters Hall of Fame.

Art is something that comes naturally, and her computerized characters emerged when Fleming purchased an iBook a few years ago. These drawings are created with AppleWorks, a finger and a track pad. "Young Masters" is Fleming's entry into the world of illustration. Personal philosophies: Motivation: fun; Inspiration: life; Perspiration: I don't believe in it; Advice: pet your cat.

Elayn J. Taylor – Saphinne, Our Storyteller

Elayn lives in Los Angeles and has appeared in film and on television including, *Bruce Almighty, Something's Gotta Give, Rules of Engagement, Dr. Doolittle 2, Sabrina, Strong Medicine, The Practice, True Blood* and more. Her stage appearances include *Rose in Fences, Gem Of The Ocean* (L.A.), *Someplace Soft To Fall* (St. Paul), and *Joe Turner* (Houston).

Diane Hsu – Flute

Diane lives in Los Angeles and performed as a concerto soloist from the age of 11 with the Seattle Philharmonic Orchestra, the Northwest Chamber Orchestra, the University of Washington Symphony and has been a selected participant in Boston University's Tanglewood Institute. Also an actress, she has appeared on film and in television in *How Stella Got Her Groove Back, Snapdragon, Totally Blonde, James Bond: License To Kill, The West Wing, Family Matters, Sunset Beach, Bloodlines* and more.

Anindo Marshall – Percussion and Vocals

Anindo began her musical and dance career in her homeland of Kenya as a vocalist, dancer and percussionist. She enjoyed a successful solo career in Europe as a vocalist, signing a recording contract with EMI Spain, and becoming known as Kenya's singing sensation. Anindo was musical and technical advisor on *Survivor Africa*, has worked on films *Kazaam, Congo* and *Ali,* and has performed with Babatunde Olatunji, and Mickey Hart of the Grateful Dead, among others. She is a certified Dunham Technique instructor and member of all female vocal group called AADAWE.

Also available from Dream A World

The Friendship Seed	*Peace In Our Land*
The Magic Eye	*Dream A World*
The Hidden Treasure	*Alphabet Affirmations*
Secrets of the Heart	*Creative World*
The Invisible Power	*A Child's Spirit*
This Little Light	*Happy Happy Kwanzaa*

www.dreamaworld.com